# DOCTOR JOKES

Compiled by Pam Rosenberg • Illustrated by Mernie Gallagher-Cole

# The Child's World®

Published by The Child's World®
1980 Lookout Drive
Mankato, MN 56003-1705
800-599-READ
www.childsworld.com

The Child's World®: Mary Berendes, Publishing Director
Editorial Directions, Inc.: E. Russell Primm, Editorial
Director; Lucia Raatma, Copyeditor and Proofreader;
Jennifer Zeiger and Joshua Gregory, Editorial Assistants
The Design Lab: Design and production

Library of Congress Cataloging-in-Publication Data
Doctor jokes / compiled by Pam Rosenberg ;
illustrated by Mernie Gallagher-Cole.
     p. cm.
  ISBN 978-1-60253-517-6 (library bound : alk. paper)
1. Medicine—Juvenile humor. 2. Physicians—Juvenile
humor. I. Rosenberg, Pam. II. Gallagher-Cole, Mernie.
III. Title.
  PN6231.M4D63 2010
  818'.602083561—dc22          2010002048

Printed in the United States of America
Mankato, Minnesota
December 2010
PA02082

## ABOUT THE AUTHOR

Pam Rosenberg is the author of more than 50 books for children. She lives near Chicago, Illinois, with her husband and two children.

## ABOUT THE ILLUSTRATOR

Mernie Gallagher-Cole lives in Pennsylvania with her husband and two children. She has illustrated many books for The Child's World®.

# TABLE
## OF
## CONTENTS

# AT THE DOCTOR'S OFFICE

**DOCTOR:** Do you always snore?
**PATIENT:** Only when I sleep.

**PATIENT:** Doctor, I can't get to sleep.
**DOCTOR:** Sit on the edge of the bed and you'll soon drop off.

4

**DOCTOR:** Nurse, did you take the patient's temperature?

**NURSE:** Why no, Doctor. Is it missing?

........................................................

**RECEPTIONIST:** The doctor is so funny that she'll soon have you in stitches.

**PATIENT:** I hope not. I just came in for a checkup.

........................................................

**PATIENT:** Doctor, will you give me something for this cold?

**DOCTOR:** Why should I? I already have a cold!

........................................................

**DOCTOR:** What happened to you, Linda?

**LINDA:** Well, Doctor, you told me to take the medicine for three days and then skip a day. All that skipping wore me out!

........................................................

**DOCTOR:** Are you an organ donor?

**PATIENT:** No, but I once gave an old piano to the Salvation Army.

**PATIENT:** Doctor, I have a problem. I keep forgetting things.
**DOCTOR:** How long have you had this problem?
**PATIENT:** What problem?

**MOTHER:** Doctor, you've got to help my daughter! All she does is scratch herself and swing from trees!

**DOCTOR:** Don't worry. She's probably just going through a phase.

**MOTHER:** Oh, thank you, Doctor. How much do I owe you?

**DOCTOR:** Thirty bananas.

......................................................................

**PATIENT:** Doctor, when I press with my finger here, it hurts. And if I press here, it hurts, too . . . and here . . . and here . . . and here. What's wrong with me?

**DOCTOR:** You have a broken finger!

......................................................................

**RECEPTIONIST:** Doctor, there's an invisible man in your waiting room.

**DOCTOR:** Tell him I can't see him now.

**DOCTOR:** I have some bad news and some very bad news.

**PATIENT:** Well, might as well give me the bad news first.

**DOCTOR:** The lab called with your test results. You have 24 hours to live.

**PATIENT:** Twenty-four hours! That's terrible! What could be worse? What's the very bad news?

**DOCTOR:** I've been trying to reach you since yesterday.

........................................................................

A man walks into a doctor's office. He has a cucumber up his nose, a carrot in his left ear, and a banana in his right ear. "What's the matter with me?" he asks the doctor.

"You're not eating properly," the doctor replies.

**Q:** Why did the doctor give up his practice?
**A:** Because he lost his patience.

A man goes to the doctor for a checkup. He hasn't been feeling well and wants to find out if he's sick. After the checkup, the doctor comes out with the results.

"I'm afraid I have some bad news," the doctor says. "You don't have much time to live."

"Oh no, that's terrible. How long have I got?" the man asks.

"Ten . . ." says the doctor.

"Ten? Ten what? Months? Weeks? What?!" the man asks desperately.

"Ten . . . nine . . . eight . . . seven . . ."

**EMERGENCY ROOM**
**DOCTOR:** So, what brings you to the hospital?
**PATIENT:** An ambulance.

A man speaks frantically into the phone, "My wife is pregnant, and she is about to have the baby!"

"Is this her first child?" the doctor asks.

"No!" the man shouts. "This is her husband!"

......................................................................

**PATIENT:** Doctor, I've just swallowed a harmonica!
**DOCTOR:** Don't worry. It could be worse—at least you don't play the piano!

**DOCTOR, DOCTOR!**

PATIENT: Doctor, Doctor! My brother smells like fish.
DOCTOR: Poor sole!

**PATIENT:** Doctor, Doctor! You have to help me out!
**DOCTOR:** Certainly. Which way did you come in?

........................................................................

**PATIENT:** Doctor, Doctor! People keep ignoring me!
**DOCTOR:** Next.

........................................................................

**PATIENT:** Doctor, Doctor! I broke my leg in four places!
**DOCTOR:** Well, don't go back to any of them.

........................................................................

**PATIENT:** Doctor, Doctor! My son has swallowed some money! What should I do?
**DOCTOR:** Nothing. But call me if there's any change.

........................................................................

**PATIENT:** Doctor, Doctor! My daughter has swallowed a roll of film!
**DOCTOR:** Well, let's hope nothing develops.

........................................................................

**PATIENT:** Doctor, Doctor! My son has swallowed a pen! What should I do?
**DOCTOR:** Use a pencil until I get there.

# DOCTOR, DOCTOR, I THINK I'M A . . .

**PATIENT:** Doctor, Doctor! I think I'm a bee!

**DOCTOR:** Well, buzz off, I'm busy!

**PATIENT:** Doctor, Doctor! I think I'm a bell!

**DOCTOR:** Take two of these, and if it doesn't help, give me a ring.

**PATIENT:** Doctor, Doctor! I think I'm an electric eel!
**DOCTOR:** That's shocking!

.................................................

**PATIENT:** Doctor, Doctor! I think I'm invisible!
**DOCTOR:** Who said that?

.................................................

**PATIENT:** Doctor, Doctor! I feel like a pair of curtains!
**DOCTOR:** Pull yourself together.

.................................................

**PATIENT:** Doctor, Doctor! I think I'm going to die!
**DOCTOR:** Don't be silly, that's the last thing you'll do!

.................................................

**PATIENT:** Doctor, I keep thinking that I'm a dog.
**PSYCHIATRIST:** Sit on the couch and we'll talk about it.
**PATIENT:** But I'm not allowed up on the couch!

.................................................

**PSYCHIATRIST:** What's your problem?
**PATIENT:** I think I'm a chicken.
**PSYCHIATRIST:** How long has this been going on?
**PATIENT:** Ever since I was an egg.

# AT THE EYE DOCTOR'S OFFICE

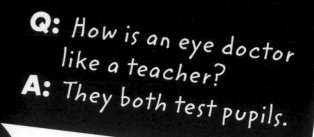
ECDFGKB
MNOPOS
ENMDOP
RSTLMP
KDFS2H
CMOWLT

A man goes to the eye doctor. The receptionist asks him why he is there. The man complains, "I keep seeing spots in front of my eyes."

The receptionist asks, "Have you ever seen a doctor?"

The man replies, "No, just spots."

16

**PATIENT:** Doctor, I think I need glasses.

**TELLER:** You certainly do. This is a bank!

·····································································

**DOCTOR:** You need new glasses.

**PATIENT:** How do you know? I haven't told you what's wrong with me yet.

**DOCTOR:** I could tell as soon as you walked in through the window!

·····································································

**KATIE:** Doctor, I always see spots in front of my eyes.

**DOCTOR:** Didn't the new glasses help?

**KATIE:** Sure. Now I see the spots much more clearly.

·····································································

**DOCTOR:** Have your eyes ever been checked?

**MATT:** No, they've always been plain brown.

·····································································

**PATIENT:** Doctor, I keep seeing double.

**DOCTOR:** Please sit on the couch.

**PATIENT:** Which one?

# SOME NURSE JOKES

**Q:** Why were the bedcovers depressed?

**A:** Because the nurse turned them down.

**Q:** What kind of music do you hear when the nurse turns down your bed?

**A:** Sheet music.

**Q:** Why did the nurse tiptoe past the medicine cabinet?

**A:** She didn't want to wake the sleeping pills.

# FEEL BETTER NOW?

**Q:** Does an apple a day keep the doctor away?

**A:** Only if you aim it well enough.

---

**Q:** What does a doctor give an injured lemon?

**A:** Lemon—ade.

---

**Q:** Why did the chicken see the doctor?

**A:** It had people pox.

---

**Q:** What did the doctor use to fix a broken heart?

**A:** Ticker tape.

**Q:** Why did the pillow go to the doctor?

**A:** He was feeling all stuffed up.

................................................................

**Q:** Did you hear about the depressed dentist?

**A:** He was a little down in the mouth.

**Q:** What did the surgeon say to the patient as he sewed him up?

**A:** That's enough out of you.

A young doctor was just setting up his first office when his secretary told him there was a man waiting to see him. The doctor wanted to make a good first impression by having the man think he was successful and very busy. He told his secretary to show the man in.

At that moment, the doctor picked up the telephone and pretended to be having a conversation with a patient. The man waited until the conversation was over. Then, the doctor put the telephone down and asked, "May I help you?"

The man replied, "No, I'm just here to connect your telephone."

............................................................

A doctor points out an X-ray to a medical student.

"As you can see," she says, "the patient limps because his feet are very arched. What would you do in a case like this?"

"Well," says the student, "I suppose I would limp, too!"

An old man sitting in the doctor's waiting room was called in to see the doctor. Grasping his cane and hunching over, he slowly made his way into the examining room.

After only a few minutes, the man emerged from the room walking completely upright! A patient who had watched him hobble into the room all hunched over stared in amazement.

"That must be a miracle doctor in there!" he exclaimed. "What treatment did he give you? What's his secret?"

The old man looked at him and said, "Well, the doctor looked me up and down, analyzed the situation, and gave me a cane that was four inches longer than the one I had been using."

**DOCTOR:** I will examine you for $20.

**PATIENT:** Go ahead, doctor. If you find it, you can have it.

**PATIENT:** Doctor, I think I'm shrinking!
**DOCTOR:** Now settle down. You'll just have to be a little patient.

24